ENERGY TRANSFERS

From
Sunlight
to
Blockbuster Movies

An Energy Journey Through the World of Light

Andrew Solway

heinemann
raintree

© 2015 Heinemann Raintree
an imprint of Capstone Global Library, LLC
Chicago, Illinois

To contact Capstone Global Library, please call 800-747-4992,
or visit our web site www.capstonepub.com

Edited by Linda Staniford and Anthony Wacholtz
Designed by Steve Mead
Original illustrations © Capstone Global Library 2015
Illustrated by HL Studios
Picture research by Eric Gohl
Production by Helen McCreath
Originated by Capstone Global Library Ltd
Printed and bound in China by CTPS

18 17 16 15 14
10 9 8 7 6 5 4 3 2 1

Library of Congress Cataloging-in-Publication Data
Solway, Andrew, author.
   From sunlight to blockbuster movies : an energy journey
through the world of light / Andrew Solway.
      pages cm.—(Energy journeys)
   Summary: "Each book in this series follows a packet of energy
along a journey. Each stage of the journey is described in
a short chapter, and we learn what alternative paths the
energy might have taken along the way. This book shows
how sunlight is turned into a movie. It explains what happens
when the sunlight reaches Earth, how its energy is stored in
fossil fuels, how this energy is then released in power stations
and used to generate electricity which is used to make light,
and finally how this light is used to make a movie. The topics
covered are illustrated with experiments, amazing facts and
scientific discoveries."— Provided by publisher.
   Includes bibliographical references and index.
   ISBN 978-1-4846-0882-1 (hb)—ISBN 978-1-4846-0887-6
(pb)—ISBN 978-1-4846-0897-5 (ebook) 1. Solar energy—Juvenile literature. 2. Power resources—Juvenile literature. 3.
Technological innovations—Juvenile literature. I. Title.

TJ810.3.S6285 2015
333.792'3—dc23   2014015611

**This book has been officially leveled by using the F&P
Text Level Gradient™ Leveling System.**

Acknowledgments
We would like to thank the following for permission to
reproduce photographs: Alamy: Flyfoto, 5, The Natural
History Museum, 16; Capstone Studio: Karon Dubke, 30, 31;
Dreamstime: Hywit Dimyadi, 26, Rastan, 14; Getty Images:
Bloomberg/Will Wintercross, 34; NASA: 9, 32, JPL-Caltech, 15,
JPL-Caltech/Steve Golden, 42; Newscom: Getty Images/AFP/
Denis Balibouse, 33, Getty Images/AFP/Saeed Khan, 36, ZUMA
Press/News-Miner/Eric Engman, 24; Science Source: Gary
Hincks, 22, GIPhotoStock, 11; Shutterstock: Andrew Zarivny, 4,
bikeriderlondon, 39, bonzodog, 25, Cessna152, 10, claffra, 23,
curraheeshutter, 20, Djaile, 41 (bottom), Fer Gregory, 37, GRei,
38, homydesign, 6, Jubal Harshaw, 17, Khakimullin Aleksandr,
cover (bottom), Mogens Trolle, 8, Ralf Gosch, 29, RonFullHD,
21, suksao, 7, Vibrant Image Studio, cover (top); Wikipedia:
TWAMWIR, 27.

We would like to thank Patrick O'Mahony for his help in the
preparation of this book.

Every effort has been made to contact copyright holders
of material reproduced in this book. Any omissions will
be rectified in subsequent printings if notice is given to
the publisher.

All the Internet addresses (URLs) given in this book were valid
at the time of going to press. However, due to the dynamic
nature of the Internet, some addresses may have changed, or
sites may have changed or ceased to exist since publication.
While the author and publisher regret any inconvenience this
may cause readers, no responsibility for any such changes can
be accepted by either the author or the publisher.

Discover amazing facts about light.

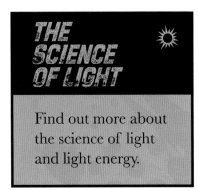

THE SCIENCE OF LIGHT

Find out more about the science of light and light energy.

LIGHT FIRSTS

Learn more about light inventions and discoveries.

1ST

Some words are shown in bold, **like this**. You can find out what they mean by looking in the glossary.

What Is Energy?

Whenever something happens, anywhere in the universe, energy is involved. It is hard to say exactly what energy is. But we would notice if there wasn't any! Without energy:

- it would be colder than the Antarctic
- it would be totally dark
- nothing would be alive
- nothing would move.

So, Earth would be pretty boring. And it would never change.

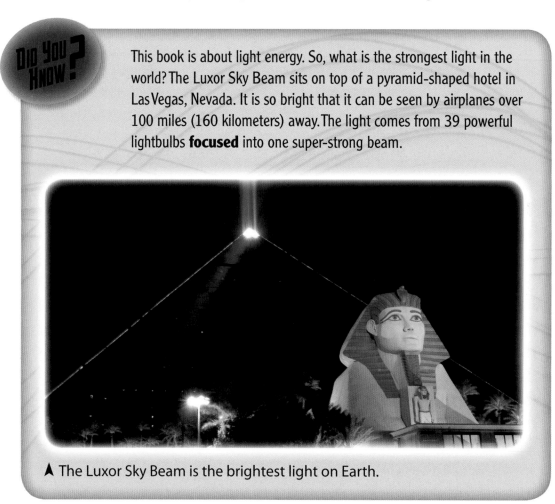

Did You Know?

This book is about light energy. So, what is the strongest light in the world? The Luxor Sky Beam sits on top of a pyramid-shaped hotel in Las Vegas, Nevada. It is so bright that it can be seen by airplanes over 100 miles (160 kilometers) away. The light comes from 39 powerful lightbulbs **focused** into one super-strong beam.

▲ The Luxor Sky Beam is the brightest light on Earth.

▲ Before launching this model plane, you must turn the propeller many times. The turning twists the rubber band and stores the rubber band's potential energy. When you let go, the propeller spins around.

All kinds of energy

There are lots of types of energy. Light, sound, movement (**kinetic energy**), heat, and electricity are all types of energy.

There are also several kinds of stored or **potential energy**. If you stretch a rubber band over a ruler, the stretched rubber band has elastic potential energy. Let go, and the rubber band flies across the room. If you put a model car at the top of a ramp, it has **gravitational** potential energy. Push it, and it will zoom down the ramp and across the floor. When you light a burner on a gas stove, it bursts into flame. The gas is full of chemical potential energy. When you light the gas, some of that energy is released.

Ever-Changing Energy

Ask an adult to light a match and hold it with tweezers until it has burned out. The energy stored in the match has gone away—hasn't it?

Actually, no. Scientists have spent many years proving an amazing thing about energy. It never goes away! Energy is INDESTRUCTIBLE! You think that the energy has gone away, but if you look carefully, you find that it is still around. It may have turned into some other kind of energy, or spread out, but it is still there.

▲ These three bikers all have gravitational potential energy. Which of them has the most?

Where does the energy go?

Let's look at an example. Imagine you are on your bike at the top of a steep hill. You have lots of gravitational potential energy. You start coasting down the hill. You go faster and faster—wheee! But then you reach the bottom, and there is a road ahead. You use the brakes, and the bike slows down, then stops.

Now you have no potential energy. But the energy hasn't disappeared. Feel the bike's brake pads. Be careful—they could be really hot! Most of the potential energy has been turned into heat, as your brake pads slowed down the bike. There might have been some sound, too, if you have squeaky brakes!

THE SCIENCE OF LIGHT

Try this experiment using a magnifying glass and a thermometer. On a sunny day, go outside and measure the temperature with the thermometer. Now put the thermometer on the ground and focus the Sun's light onto it with the magnifying glass. What happens?

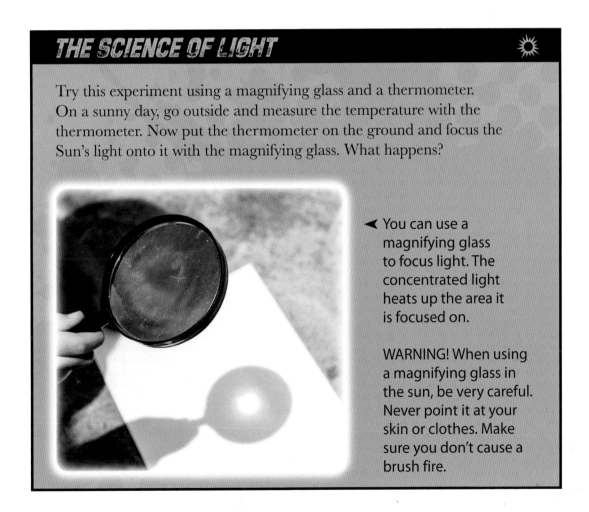

◀ You can use a magnifying glass to focus light. The concentrated light heats up the area it is focused on.

WARNING! When using a magnifying glass in the sun, be very careful. Never point it at your skin or clothes. Make sure you don't cause a brush fire.

What Is the Most Important Energy Source on Earth?

The energy journey in this book starts with our most important energy source. But this energy source isn't on Earth at all—it is 93 million miles (150 million kilometers) away!

The energy that drives almost everything that happens on Earth is sunlight. Let's look at why we need sunlight. Most obviously, the Sun lights Earth up. Sunlight also warms Earth. You can feel this heat directly on a sunny day.

The light and warmth of the Sun provide the energy for living things to grow. Plants use sunlight to make their food. This process is called **photosynthesis**. Animals cannot make their own food, so they eat either plants or other animals. So, all living things ultimately get their energy from sunlight.

▼ Lions hunt other animals, but prey animals such as zebra eat plants. The plants need sunlight, so without sunlight, lions would have no food.

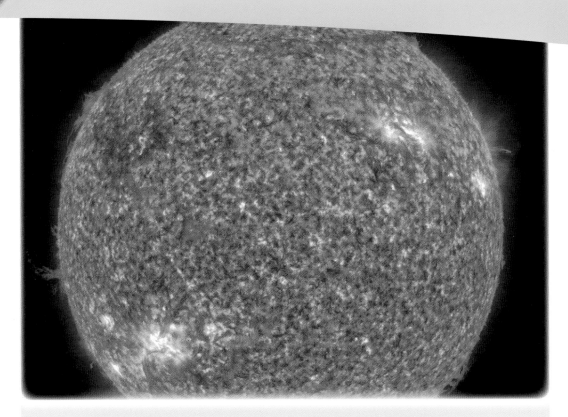

▲ This photo of the Sun was taken using a space telescope designed to show details of the surface.

Weather and landscape

Sunlight also produces Earth's weather. For example, clouds form when the Sun warms the surface of the sea, and water rises up into the air. The clouds carry the water over land, where it falls as rain or snow.

Even the shape of the land is affected by sunlight. Rain that falls on land produces rivers, which cut valleys through mountains and hills. And rocks that are warmed by sunlight in the day can crack and split when they get cold at night. Over many years, this process can wear down mountains.

A bright lightbulb in the home uses about 20 watts of energy. The sunlight that reaches Earth has enough energy to power about 8,500 trillion lightbulbs. (A trillion is one million million.)

The energy journey begins

Our energy journey begins with the Sun. Light energy pours out of the Sun in huge quantities. Some of it travels across the vast distance of space to Earth.

An important **property** of light is that it travels in straight lines. The trip to Earth takes only eight minutes, because light travels incredibly quickly—186,000 miles (300,000 kilometers) every second!

Bouncing and bending

Once the light reaches Earth, it meets all kinds of different materials. What happens then? Most materials **absorb** light. You can't shine a light through a brick wall, because the bricks absorb the light energy.

▲ The sunny side of a wall gets warmer than the side that is in shadow. The bricks absorb sunlight, and some of it is **transformed** into heat.

Light energy is a wave: a sort of vibration in space. Sunlight is a mix of waves of many different wavelengths. Different wavelengths of light have different colors and carry different amounts of energy. Violet light has the shortest wavelength and is the most energetic. Red light has the longest wavelength and has the least energy.

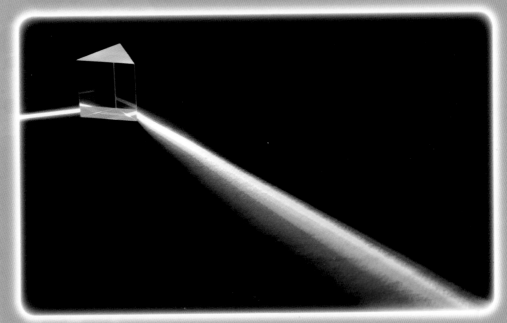

▲ When white light passes through a prism, the different wavelengths of light separate to form a rainbow of colors.

Sometimes when light rays hit an object, they bounce off the surface. This is called **reflection**. The smooth surface of a mirror is designed to reflect most of the light that hits it.

Some materials, such as glass and air, are **transparent**. If light passes from one transparent material into another—for example, from air into glass—the light changes direction slightly. This bending of light is called **refraction**. The lenses in eyeglasses, binoculars, telescopes, and microscopes all work using refraction.

USING A RAY BOX TO INVESTIGATE REFLECTION

A ray box is a way to create a thin beam of light. You can use it to show the path of a light ray reflected from a mirror.

You will need:
- a shoebox
- scissors
- a flashlight
- duct tape or other strong tape
- paper
- a small mirror
- sticky putty
- colored pencils
- a ruler.

Before you begin…

- Ask an adult to cut a thin slit, about 2 inches (5 centimeters) long, in one end of the shoebox. In the other end of the shoebox, ask the adult to cut a hole for your flashlight.
- Push the flashlight through the hole so that it is pointing toward the slit. Tape it in place.
- Put a piece of paper flat in front of the shoebox at the end with the thin slit.

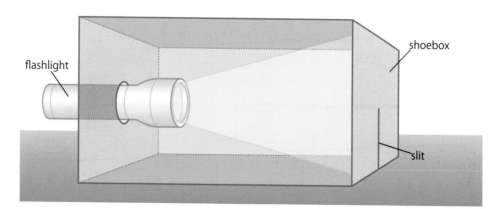

flashlight

shoebox

slit

- Turn on the flashlight and darken the room. You should see a thin beam of light coming out of the slit in the shoebox. You now have a ray box!

Making it work

1 Draw a line on the paper that follows the light ray from the ray box.

2 Use sticky putty to stick a mirror in front of the light ray, facing toward the ray box.

3 What happens to the light ray? Draw lines to mark the front of the mirror and where the light ray goes.

4 Turn the mirror so that it is at an angle to the ray box.

5 Mark the new mirror angle and the new light ray on the paper, in a different color.

6 Try the mirror at two other angles. Mark the line of the mirror and the light ray in two different colors.

7 When you have finished, you will have diagrams that show how light is reflected from a mirror.

Alternative journeys

The Sun **radiates** energy in all directions. Only a tiny part of the energy it produces falls on Earth. The rest radiates out into space. If it isn't absorbed by a dust cloud or a space rock, the energy could keep traveling for millions of years.

Ancient light

If you look up into the sky on a clear night, you will see light that has traveled for years and years from distant suns. These are stars.

One of the best-known **constellations** in the sky is Orion. The stars in Orion are very, very far away. The light from Orion's stars traveled across space for hundreds of years before finally reaching Earth.

Alnilam

▲ The stars in the constellation of Orion are very far away. The middle star in Orion's belt is called Alnilam. Light takes 1,340 years to travel from Alnilam to Earth.

▲ This is an artist's idea of how the Sun might look from a distant planet.

So, imagine aliens standing on a planet billions and billions of miles from Earth. They look up into the sky one night and notice a star shining brightly in the darkness. They could be seeing light from our Sun, which has traveled across space for years and years.

THE SCIENCE OF LIGHT

How does the Sun produce the energy to shine so brightly? The Sun is an enormous ball of gas. The gas is the fuel that keeps it going. The heart of the Sun is like a huge nuclear power station. **Nuclear energy** is the energy locked up in the nuclei (centers) of **atoms**. This is the energy that is released in the Sun.

Why Is Sunlight from the Past Still Important Today?

The Sun has been lighting and warming Earth for over 4 billion years. So, the sunlight we are following in our journey could have reached Earth millions of years ago. We have seen already that energy is indestructible. So, energy that reached Earth millions of years ago could still be here!

▼ During the Cretaceous period, around 100 million years ago, dinosaurs were the dominant land animals.

Energy for plants

Imagine sunlight that reached Earth about 100 million years ago. It fell on a warm, shallow sea close to the coastline. This sea had microscopic plants floating in the water. Some of the sunlight was absorbed by a chemical called **chlorophyll** inside these plants. Chlorophyll is the **pigment** that gives plant leaves their green color.

Capturing sunlight in chlorophyll is the first stage in the process of photosynthesis. The energy from the sunlight does some complicated chemistry inside the cells of these microscopic plants. This chemistry turns water from the sea, and carbon dioxide from the air, into sugars. The sugars are food for the plants. During this stage of the energy journey, sunlight has been captured and stored as chemical potential energy.

The microscopic plants and creatures that float in the sea and drift with the sea currents are called **plankton**. They are the basic food for everything else in the ocean. One hundred million years ago, tiny plant-like creatures called **diatoms** were the most important type of plankton. They produced food for everything, from shrimps to huge sea reptiles.

➤ These are diatoms under a microscope. They often have hard outer skeletons that are beautifully patterned.

Buried and cooked

When diatoms and other plankton die, they sink to the seabed and are buried in mud. Over many years, a thick layer of mud builds up. This mud is full of the remains of plankton.

More time passes, and the layer of mud becomes buried under sand and other materials. As the mud layer is buried further, it gets hotter. The mud is also crushed by the weight of the other materials above it. This combination of heat and pressure "cooks" the mud.

Changes in the cooking

When you bake a cake, the flour, eggs, and other ingredients change. During millions of years of "cooking," the plankton-rich mud from the seabed changes, too. It becomes oil and gas.

As oil and gas form, they are crushed into all the tiny holes and gaps in the rock layers. Over time, the oil and gas gradually rise up through these rock layers. Eventually, they reach a rock layer that is **impermeable**. This means that there are no holes and gaps in the rock. The oil and gas can't move through this layer. They are trapped here, and they build up to form oil fields and gas fields.

The energy in the microscopic plants is locked up in the chemicals produced by photosynthesis. During the "cooking" process, the chemicals change, but the energy remains stored inside them. In fact, energy is added during the "cooking."

Only the top layer of the Earth is solid and cool. About 19 miles (30 kilometers) below the surface, the temperature is between 5,400 and 9,000 degrees Fahrenheit (3,000 and 5,000 degrees Celsius), which is hot enough to melt rock. The temperature at the center of the Earth is around 12,600 degrees Fahrenheit (7,000 degrees Celsius).

▼ These diagrams show how oil fields and gas fields form.

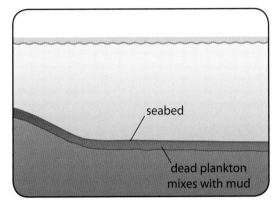

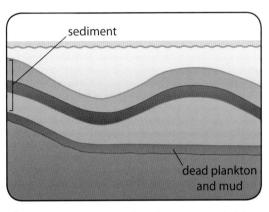

▲ 1. A layer of mud and organic material builds up on the seabed.

▲ 2. Other layers of sediment are laid down above the mud.

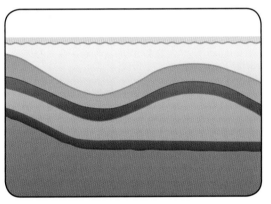

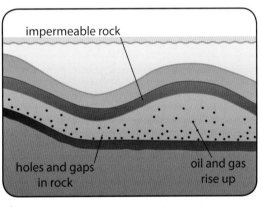

▲ 3. The mud layer is "cooked" by a mix of heat and pressure. Oil and gas form.

▲ 4. Oil and gas rise up through the rocks above.

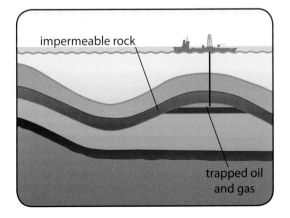

◄ 5. The oil and gas reach a layer of impermeable rock. They collect in one place to form an oil field.

Oil and gas

The energy stored in the oil and gas remains trapped underground, beneath the sea, for many years. Then, an oil company discovers the oil field and sets up a drilling rig. The rig has a large drilling platform on the sea surface. From here, a long drill goes down to the seabed and drills deep into the rocks. Eventually, it reaches the oil and gas far below.

▲ This is a modern deep-sea oil drilling rig. The large flare is waste gas being burned off.

The first substance to come up from the seabed is gas, because it is lighter. Then, the heavier oil comes to the surface. In some places, there is not very much gas, and so it is not worth collecting. Here it is burned off or used on the oil rig. In other places, the trapped energy is nearly all gas, and it is definitely worth collecting!

The oil and gas are carried away from the drilling rig in pipes or in huge tankers. They go to a **refinery** to be turned into gasoline, diesel, and other useful products.

An oil refinery

Crude oil is a mix of many chemicals, from light gases to heavy tars. In a refinery, these substances are separated into different products. The most important of them are:

- gasoline: about 42% of the total
- diesel: about 22% of the total
- jet fuel: about 9% of the total
- fuel oil (for heating buildings): about 5% of the total.

LIGHT FIRSTS

1ST

The first oil wells to produce oil for fuel were in North America in the 1850s. In 1858, Canadian James Williams discovered a well in Oil Springs, Ontario, in Canada. A year later, in 1859, Edwin Drake discovered oil near Titusville, Pennsylvania.

▲ In an oil refinery, the different substances in the crude oil are separated in the tall towers.

Alternative journeys

Only a tiny fraction of the sunlight falling on Earth 100 million years ago was stored in fuels such as oil and gas. What happened to the rest?

Most of the energy falling on the sea would have been absorbed, which would warm the sea surface. Some sunlight would be reflected back into the air. Some of the warmth from the sea would also rise up into the air.

Earth is always losing heat and light energy into space, because it is so much warmer than its surroundings. So, some of the sunlight falling on Earth is radiated back out into space.

▲ When sunlight reaches Earth, some is absorbed by the ground, some is absorbed by the air, and some is reflected back into space.

Sunlight on the land

If the sunlight had fallen on the land instead of the sea, it could have been captured by land plants. Around 100 million years ago, the first flowering plants were flourishing on Earth. When they died, they would have **decomposed** quickly and become part of the soil, instead of turning into **fossil fuels**.

Coal, oil, and gas are all fossil fuels. They formed from plants and animals that lived millions of years ago. Most of Earth's coal was formed around 300 million years ago, when huge areas were covered by swamps. The coal formed from tree-like plants that died and rotted very slowly in the swampy ground. Oil and gas mostly formed in the sea, from much smaller living things.

▲ In some areas, there are coal deposits close to the surface. The coal can be dug out using huge excavators like this one.

How Do Power Stations Produce Electricity?

*In the next stage of the energy journey, some of the oil is sent to a power station. It becomes the fuel for a large **furnace**. When the oil burns, the chemical energy that has been stored in it for millions of years is released at last.*

Burning is a chemical reaction. The chemicals in the oil are turned mainly into a gas, carbon dioxide. This releases a lot of energy as heat. The temperature in the furnace reaches over 930 degrees Fahrenheit (500 degrees Celsius).

▼ This is a furnace in a fossil fuel power station. The burning fuel gets extremely hot, but it also produces a bright white light.

▲ These are the smoke stacks and cooling towers of an oil-fired power station.

Not all the energy released from the fuel becomes heat. The furnace burns brightly, producing light energy. And the burning fuel makes a roaring noise, so some of the energy is transformed into sound.

What does the heat do?

The heat produced by the furnace is not used to warm the building. Many thin pipes run through the furnace, each one carrying flowing water. As the water flows through the pipes and passes through the furnace, it turns into high-pressure steam. The energy of the burning fuel remains as heat, but some of the heat is **transferred** from the burning fuel to the water.

DID YOU KNOW?
Power stations using fossil fuels (coal, oil, or gas) produce nearly 80 percent of the world's electricity. In all these power stations, most of the burning fuel is turned into carbon dioxide. There is strong evidence that higher levels of carbon dioxide in the air are trapping more heat in Earth's **atmosphere**. This is leading to **global warming**, and Earth's climate is gradually getting warmer.

Turning the turbines

The high-pressure steam from the pipes in the furnace is used to power a machine called a **steam turbine**. As the steam goes into the turbine, it is traveling at about 1,000 miles per hour (1,600 kilometers per hour). The steam pushes against the blades of a set of large fans and sets them spinning.

The steam loses heat and speed as it pushes against the turbine blades. The energy of the steam is transferred to the turbine blades, which gain kinetic energy.

▲ This photo of a steam turbine being built shows the multiple turbines that fill the inside.

Gas turbines

In some smaller power stations, burning gas is used to spin turbine blades instead of steam. Gas turbines are similar to the jet engines used in aircraft. They work at much hotter temperatures than steam turbines. In some power stations, the hot gases that spin the gas turbine blades are then used to heat water, so they can also power a steam turbine. This is a very efficient system. It turns more of the energy from the fuel into kinetic energy in the spinning turbine blades.

Did You Know?

The first modern steam turbine was built in 1884 by the British engineer Charles Parsons. In 1895, three of his turbines were used to provide electric lighting for the city of Cambridge, England. Parsons also built a boat called *Turbinia*, which was powered by steam turbines. When it was built in 1894, *Turbinia* was the fastest ship in the world. It could reach speeds of almost 35 knots (40 miles per hour/64 kilometers per hour).

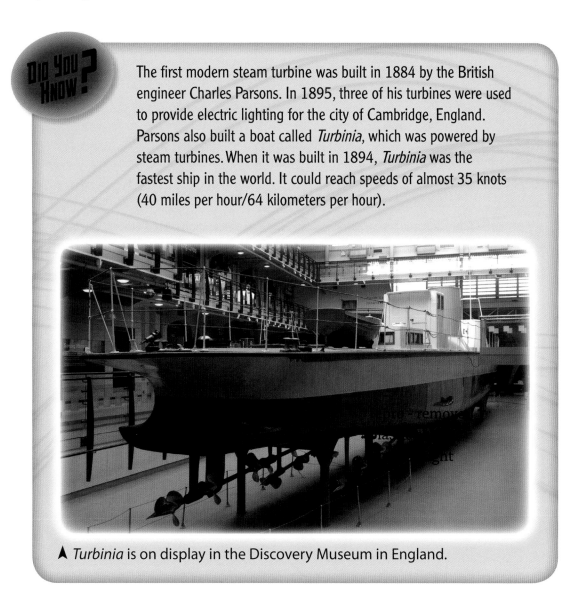

▲ *Turbinia* is on display in the Discovery Museum in England.

Generating electricity

So far in the power station, the chemical energy from the oil has been transformed into heat, and then into kinetic energy. How does the kinetic energy become electricity?

Generators

Power stations use **generators** to produce electricity. The main parts are:

- a magnet or magnets
- wire
- kinetic energy.

Any magnet has an invisible **magnetic field** around it. Scientists in the 1800s found that if you move a wire through a magnetic field, an electric current flows in the wire. This seems very straightforward.

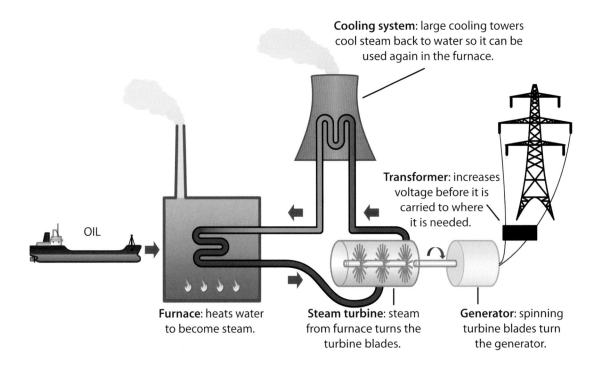

Cooling system: large cooling towers cool steam back to water so it can be used again in the furnace.

Transformer: increases voltage before it is carried to where it is needed.

OIL

Furnace: heats water to become steam.

Steam turbine: steam from furnace turns the turbine blades.

Generator: spinning turbine blades turn the generator.

▲ This diagram shows how a power station makes electricity.

▲ In the future, wind turbines could produce electricity using superconducting generators.

In reality, it is not quite that simple. Moving one wire in a magnetic field produces a very tiny electric current. For a powerful generator, you need a coil with thousands of turns of wire. The wire is coiled tightly around a **rotor**, which spins very quickly in a strong magnetic field.

Spinning electricity

You need a lot of energy to spin a huge coil of wire in a magnetic field. This is where the turbine comes in. The spinning turbine blades turn a shaft, which turns the rotor of the generator. As the rotor spins, a strong electric current is generated. The kinetic energy from the turbine is transformed into electrical energy.

DID YOU KNOW?
At very low temperatures, some materials can become **superconductors**. Electricity can flow through them very easily. Researchers are experimenting with using superconductors to build electricity generators that are small, light, and extremely powerful. Two possible uses for these are lighter, more streamlined ships and powerful, efficient wind turbines.

MAKING A SIMPLE GENERATOR

In this experiment, you can see how moving a magnet through a coil of wire produces an electric current.

You will need:
- **a film canister case or other closed plastic tube**
- **a small, strong magnet**
- **enameled wire (magnet wire)**
- **two short wires with clips on each end**
- **electrical tape**
- **an LED lightbulb**
- **cardboard.**

Before you begin…

Look at the photo below to see the parts you need for your generator. You can use any kind of magnet that will fit in the plastic tube. You will get the best results with a strong magnet.

Making it work

1 Put the magnet in the plastic tube and tape it shut. Cut out two cardboard rings that will slide onto the tube. Slide the rings onto the tube and tape them on. Wind the thin wire between the rings, at least 200 times. Keep a short length of wire free at each end.

2 Use the wires with clips to connect the ends of the wire coil to the LED lightbulb. Your generator is ready!

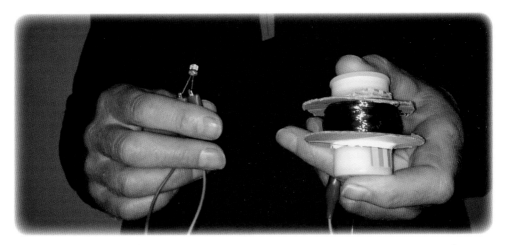

3 To make your generator work, you have to make the magnet move through the coil of wire. To do this, hold the bulb in one hand, and with the other hand shake the plastic tube up and down. The LED lightbulb should flash on and off.

What happened?

In the power station generator, the energy to produce electricity comes from the steam turbine. Where does the energy come from in this simple generator? You could change your generator and see what the effects are. What happens if you add more coils of wire? What happens if you use stronger magnets?

Alternative journeys

The sunlight that fell on ancient Earth took around 100 million years to transform from light into electricity. Today, we have devices that can do this in a fraction of a second.

Solar panels (**photovoltaic cells**, or PV cells) are able to convert sunlight directly into electricity. The main part of a PV cell is a layer of a **semiconductor** material such as silicon. Semiconductors are the main materials in microchips and electronics. The semiconductor is specially treated so that when light falls on one side of the cell, an electric current is produced.

A single solar cell produces only a small amount of electricity, so cells are arranged in groups, or **arrays**. A solar panel is an array of PV cells.

▲ The Van Allen Probes are two satellites that orbit Earth measuring radiation levels. The electricity that powers the measuring instruments comes from the eight solar panels on each satellite.

▲ In 2010, the aircraft *Solar Impulse* made the longest nonstop flight by a solar-powered aircraft up to that time. It flew for over 26 hours using the power from its solar panels. Electricity produced during the day was stored in batteries, which kept the aircraft flying all night.

Energy on the move

The crude oil that came from under the ocean was not all used for power-station fuel. Some of it was turned into gasoline or diesel fuel. These fuels provide energy for cars, trucks, ships, and other kinds of transportation. They all have engines that turn heat energy into kinetic energy.

1ST

LIGHT FIRSTS

The first PV cell was made by Bell Laboratories in the United States in 1954. The first major use for PV cells was to power space satellites. The satellite Telstar 1, launched in 1962, was designed to bounce telephone, radio, and TV signals across the Atlantic Ocean. It had PV cells all over its surface. Later satellites had the PV cells on long "wings" that could be turned to face the sunlight.

How Do We Turn Light into Electricity and Then Back to Light Again?

In the final stage of our energy journey, the energy that started off as sunlight millions of years earlier finally becomes light energy once more.

Traveling through the network

Electricity leaves power stations at high **voltage**. This is the best way to carry electricity long distances. When it reaches the place where it will be used, a **transformer** reduces the voltage to lower levels.

The energy in this journey is produced very early in the morning, when demand for electricity is low. At this time, the electricity is not needed, so it has to be stored. It is sent to a pumped storage power station, where it is changed once more.

➤ This is inside the pumped storage power station at Dinorwig in Wales. The photo shows the top of one of the water turbines.

The largest pumped storage power station in the world is Bath County Pumped Storage Station in Virginia, with a capacity of about 3,000 megawatts. Dinorwig Power Station in Wales, United Kingdom, is the largest power station of its kind in Europe, with a maximum capacity of about 1,700 megawatts. It has 10 miles (16 kilometers) of underground tunnels that run deep below a mountain.

Storing electricity

In a pumped storage power station, electricity is used to drive a turbine that works as a pump. The turbine pumps water from a **reservoir** at the bottom of a hill or mountain to a second reservoir at the top. In the pump, the electricity is transformed into kinetic energy. This kinetic energy is then transferred from the pump to the water. As the water is pumped up the mountain, the kinetic energy is gradually changed to gravitational potential energy. When the water settles down in the reservoir at the top of the mountain, all its energy is potential energy.

Later in the day, there is a bigger demand for electricity. Water from the top reservoir is allowed to flow downhill into the bottom one. As it does so, it turns the same turbine as before. Instead of being a pump, the turbine now turns a generator to produce electricity.

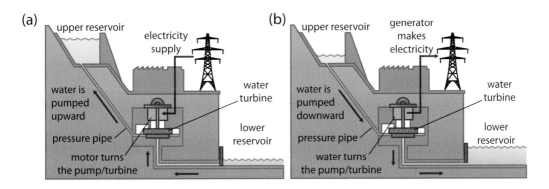

▲ This diagram shows how pumped storage works: (a) water is pumped to the upper reservoir, and (b) electricity is generated.

Light and movement

Now our energy journey takes us to a movie theater. Inside, a blockbuster movie is showing. It's full of noise and action. The energy for all this excitement comes from electricity.

▲ People line up for tickets to see the latest blockbuster.

The movie is shown using a projector. Inside the projector, the electricity does several things. It flows through a projector bulb, which is a glass tube with a small amount of gas inside it. The electricity causes the gas to glow, producing a bright light.

Electricity is also used to power an electric motor. This works like a generator in reverse. In a generator, turning a magnet inside a coil of wire produces an electric current. In a motor, sending a current through the coil of wire makes the magnet turn.

◄ This is an old movie projector with a spool of film. The powerful lightbulb inside the projector produces heat as well as light. The large rectangular block on the right is a heat sink, which helps to cool the projector down.

The motor is used to turn the spools that feed the film past the light. A lens focuses the pictures from the film onto the movie screen.

Sound as well

Electricity also drives the loudspeakers that produce the sound. Loudspeakers use a combination of a coil and a magnet, just like a motor. But instead of producing a turning motion, the magnet causes vibrations in the loudspeaker cone. This produces vibrations in the air that we hear as sounds.

DID YOU KNOW? The latest projectors don't use film or lightbulbs. All the picture information is stored on a computer. The computer uses the information to control three lasers: one red, one green, and one blue. It "paints" the images onto the screen, mixing the light to make a whole range of colors and shapes.

Powering the senses

The energy journey is almost over, but not quite. The pictures and sounds travel from the screen to the eyes and ears of the people in the audience. Maybe you are one of them!

Eyes and ears

You see the pictures on the movie screen with your eyes. The light goes into your eyes through a hole called the pupil. Behind the pupil is a lens, which focuses the light onto a small area of the retina at the back of your eye. The retina is covered in light-sensitive cells. When light falls on them, they produce electrical energy. This electrical energy creates a **nerve signal**, which travels through nerves to your brain.

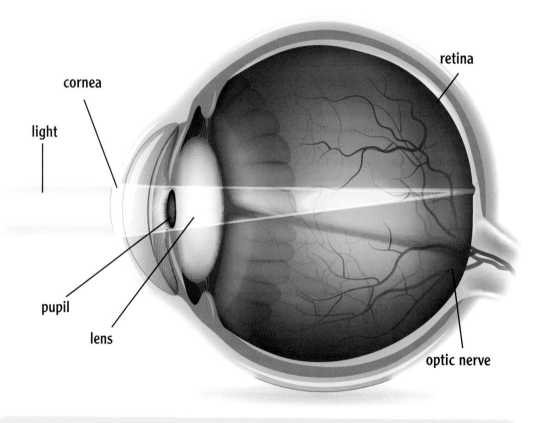

cornea

light

retina

pupil

lens

optic nerve

▲ This diagram shows how the eye works.

Your ears are a bit like loudspeakers working in reverse. The sounds from the movie cause the eardrum in your ear to vibrate. This vibration produces nerve signals in cells inside your ear. Like the signals from your eyes, these signals travel to your brain.

Making sense of it all

Your brain takes the information coming from your eyes and your ears and makes sense of them. The electrical signals from your eyes become pictures, and the signals from your ears become sounds. Electrical nerve signals turn into car chases and loud explosions!

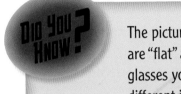

The pictures on a movie screen are only two-dimensional (2-D). They are "flat" and have no depth. In a three-dimensional (3-D) movie, the glasses you have to wear trick your eyes. They show each eye slightly different images. Your brain puts the two images together and sees the image as 3-D. Now the image has depth as well as height and width.

▲ An audience at a 3-D movie needs special glasses to get the 3-D effect.

MAKING A PINHOLE CAMERA

Although a pinhole camera has no lens, it works in a similar way to a camera or your eye. The camera is light-tight. This means that no light can get in, except for a small pinhole at one end. The pinhole acts to focus the light from the surroundings, in a similar way to a lens.

You will need:
- **an empty potato chip can**
- **a ruler and pen**
- **a sharp craft knife, and an adult to use it**
- **a thumb tack**
- **tracing paper or wax paper**
- **duct tape or other light-tight tape.**

Making it work

1 Take the plastic lid off the potato chip can and wipe it out. Measure 2 inches (5 centimeters) from the bottom of the can and mark it all around.

2 Ask an adult to cut through the can where you have marked it.

3 Use the thumb tack to make a small, round hole in the metal bottom of the can.

4 Cut a circle of tracing paper the same size as the lid of the can. Put the tracing paper inside the lid, and put the lid on the short, bottom part of the can.

5 Use the duct tape to tape the longer part of the can back on top of the short end, on the lid side.

6 Go outside on a bright day. Put the open end of the can up to your eye, making sure to block out as much light as possible (you could put a blanket over your head). You will see an upside-down image of the scene on the tracing paper screen inside the can.

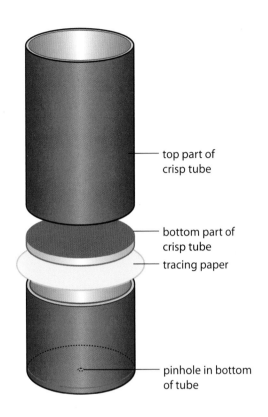

top part of crisp tube

bottom part of crisp tube

tracing paper

pinhole in bottom of tube

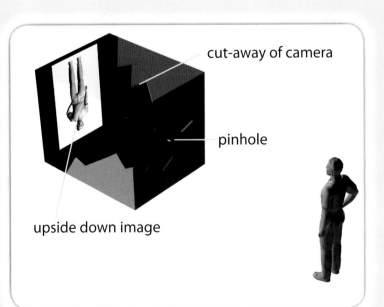

cut-away of camera

pinhole

upside down image

◄ If you have some photographic paper or film, you can make a simple pinhole camera that takes photos.

What Have We Learned About Light and Energy?

This energy journey started with light energy at the Sun's surface. It ended millions of miles away and millions of years later with light and sound in a movie theater on Earth. In between, the energy was transformed into chemical potential energy, heat, kinetic energy, electrical energy, gravitational potential energy, electrical energy a second time, then kinetic energy, light, and sound.

▲ Some of the sunlight radiated from the Sun over 100 million years ago is still traveling through space.

In this energy journey, we have learned a few things. For example:

- Light is a kind of wave that can travel very quickly across space or through the air.
- Light can be absorbed, reflected, or bent (refracted).
- Plants can use light energy to make food.
- Sometimes the chemical energy in plants can be stored in fossil fuels.
- We generate most of our electricity in power stations that use fossil fuels.
- If electricity can't be used right away, it can be stored as gravitational potential energy.
- A movie projector transforms electrical energy into a mixture of light, sound, and kinetic energy.
- Our senses turn light and sound into electrical nerve impulses.

A continuing journey

The most important thing to remember is that energy can't be created or destroyed. The energy in this journey was not created in the Sun. Before it became sunlight, it was chemical potential energy in a hydrogen gas cloud. The sound and light energy at the end of the journey does not disappear completely. Most of it turns into heat, which warms up the movie theater. Somewhere, right now, the energy journey is continuing…

Stage of journey	Type of energy
Sun	light
Plants	chemical potential energy
Fossil fuel	chemical potential energy
Extraction	chemical potential energy
Refining	chemical potential energy
Power station furnace	heat energy
Steam turbine	kinetic energy
Generator	electricity
Pumped storage	gravitational potential energy
Regeneration	electricity
Projector	light, sound, kinetic energy
Audience	electricity (nerve signals)

▲ This table shows how the energy changed along its journey from the Sun.

Glossary

absorb take in or soak up

array (solar) group of solar cells arranged and connected so that they work together

atmosphere air around us

atom basic building block of matter

chlorophyll green pigment found in plants that absorbs light. It plays an important part in the process of photosynthesis.

constellation group of stars that makes a pattern in the sky

decompose rot

diatom microscopic, plant-like living things with a hard outer cell wall

focus bring light rays together to one point, or to form an image

fossil fuel any fuel that is made from the remains of long-dead living things. Coal, oil, and natural gas are all fossil fuels.

furnace device or container that is heated to a very high temperature

generator machine for producing electricity

global warming increase in the average temperature of Earth, which scientists think is due to the increase of carbon dioxide in the atmosphere

gravitational relating to gravity, the force that attracts objects toward one another

impermeable not allowing liquid or gas to pass through

kinetic energy movement energy

magnetic field invisible area around a magnet where it exerts a force on another magnet or on a magnetic material such as iron

nerve signal electrical pulse along a nerve that carries information

nuclear energy energy that is held in the nucleus (center) of an atom

photosynthesis way in which plants make sugars from light energy, carbon dioxide gas (from the air), and water

photovoltaic (PV) cell device that converts light directly into electricity

pigment colored chemical

plankton small or microscopic living things that live in the ocean

potential energy energy that is stored in some way

property (physical) way in which something behaves

radiate spread out from a central point

refinery chemical factory that separates the many different substances in crude oil

reflection when light bounces off a smooth surface

refraction when light changes direction as it moves from one transparent material into another

reservoir artificial lake, usually formed by damming a river

rotor part of a machine that spins around

semiconductor material, such as silicon, germanium, or gallium, that is used in electronic devices and in photovoltaic cells

steam turbine machine that uses a jet of steam to turn one or more many-bladed fans

superconductor material that at very low temperatures allows electricity to flow with hardly any resistance

transfer (energy) when energy stays in the same form (for example, kinetic energy), but is passed from one substance to another

transform (energy) when energy changes from one form to another— for example, from light into chemical energy

transformer device used to change the voltage and current of an electricity supply

transparent allowing light to pass through

voltage force or "pressure" of an electric current. The higher the voltage, the more electrical energy is involved.

Find Out More

Books

Carlson Berne, Emma. *Bright! Light Energy* (Energy Everywhere). New York: PowerKids, 2013.

Claybourne, Anna. *Secrets of Light* (Science Secrets). New York: Marshall Cavendish Benchmark, 2011.

Hartman, Eve, and Wendy Meshbesher. *Fossil Fuels* (Sci-Hi). Chicago: Raintree, 2010.

Morris, Neil. *Fossil Fuels* (Energy Now and In the Future). Mankato, Minn.: Smart Apple Media, 2010.

Solway, Andrew. *The Scientists Behind Energy* (Sci-Hi Scientists). Chicago: Raintree, 2011.

Web sites

www.diyphotography.net/23-pinhole-cameras-that-you-can-build-at-home
On this web site, there are 23 different pinhole cameras. One of them is made from a peanut!

www.kidskonnect.com/subjectindex/15-educational/science/495-light.html
Find out more about light on this web site, which has lots of useful links.

www.scientificamerican.com/article/how-does-solar-power-work
Find out more about solar cells and solar power on this web site.

www.youtube.com/watch?v=zk2YL46ewo0
This is a video showing more information about the Bath County Pumped Storage Station in Virginia.

Places to visit

The Exploratorium

Pier 15, San Francisco, California 94111

The Exploratorium is a great place to visit to find out about any science or technology topic, including light, and to have fun with hands-on exhibits.

www.exploratorium.edu

George Eastman House International Museum of Photography and Film

900 East Avenue, Rochester, New York 14607

Learn more about photography and movies at this museum.

www.eastmanhouse.org

Further research

Think about the different sections of the energy journey in this book. Which part would you most want to learn more about?

- You could do more research into the Sun, our most important energy source. There are many questions you could ask. How does the Sun make our weather? How does it produce ocean currents? How do plants produce food from light? What about the diatoms and other algae that produce food for ocean creatures?
- Maybe you are more interested in how tiny plants floating in the sea can turn into oil and gas? Perhaps you could find out more about what Earth was like 100 million years ago? Or learn more about the tremendous heat in Earth's core? Or perhaps you could find out more about how we find and extract oil and gas?
- Power stations are the way that we make electricity, which is our main source of power. Can you find out more about other kinds of power stations, such as nuclear power plants or wind farms? Which kinds of power are best for reducing global warming?
- Maybe you are interested in a more practical project? Perhaps you could try making a generator that uses spinning magnets to make electricity? Or maybe you could make a pinhole camera that actually records images on film?

Index